AND THE BEAT
GOES ON

RENEE E. JONES

Renee E. Jones

ISBN: 978-0988179615

Published by REJ Enterprises, LLC

Website: www.iamreneejones.com

Cover Design by: thatsladymillz@gmail.com
Editing by: LaKeisha Rainey-Collins

Printed in the United States of America

DEDICATIONS

I dedicate this book in loving memory of my son, Trevin D'Shawn Reddick. Although the pain of losing you lingers on, I have found my strength to share our amazing story with the world. Every time I gave up along the way, I was able to latch on to the words you gave me over the years, – "Come on ma, you got this!" The nineteen years I had with you will be treasured in my heart forever. I love you to the end.

I also dedicate this book to every parent who has had the agonizing task of burying a child. You have the strength within you to keep smiling; keep laughing; and keep living. Your child would have wanted that for you.

Last, but not least, I dedicate this book to Organ Donor Families. The bitter-sweetness of being a part of this family can only be understood by those of us that are already here. Because of our willingness to share in such a painful moment, others now have a second chance to live their lives.

Renee E. Jones

Our loved ones are not gone, they live on. Stand strong and continue to share your story, it can be healing for your soul.

ACKNOWLEDGEMENTS

With God, all things are possible! Just when I thought I would not make it, Jesus stepped in right on time and rescued me.

To my children and grandchildren, you mean the world to me. I cherish every moment we spend together - you give me a reason to keep smiling, shining and living life on purpose.

To my entire family who stood by me and continues to do so during the most painful event of my life, thank you. I love you all dearly.

To Trevin's organ recipients, may our Heavenly Father forever bless and keep you as you live your new life.

My husband, my rock, and earthly king - I don't know why you love me so, but I'm sure glad you do. Thank you for always protecting me and giving me the courage to close my eyes and fall backwards without fear of landing safely in your arms. My love for you runs deep.

Renee E. Jones

ANGEL IN OUR HEARTS

Although you have gone away from our presence,
we still hold you close and near;
You were a soul so precious, a soul so dear.

Even though the pain cuts deep within our hearts;
the love we feel for you will never depart.

You are gone so soon as our angel on earth;
so much pain, so much hurt.

But, we stand strong and we stand tall;
resting on our faith and knowing,
you are now an angel in our hearts.

© 2012

CONTENTS

Renee E. Jones

INTRODUCTION

Has life ever thrown you a curve ball that came so hard, so fast, and completely unexpected that it knocked you off your feet, took your breath away, and changed your entire life? Not metaphorically, but literally. Have you ever experienced such a tragedy that made you feel caught up in a whirlwind of emotions, while simultaneously and seemingly having an out-of-body experience? How about this: Have you ever encountered a pain that ran so deep and excruciating that you felt there's no way to recover from it?

Yeah? Then, you're not alone...so have I.

I lost my son on October 31, 2011.

When I received the news that my son had been shot, I had no idea how our lives would be affected because of it. I was not prepared for the chain of events that followed, and, even to this day, I find myself wondering how in the world I survived such emotional trauma.

When someone you hold dear is tragically and senselessly taken away from you, you experience a plethora of emotions – sadness, anger, hurt, resentment, hatred, and the list goes on.

So what do you do with those feelings? How do you go on with life after such a loss?

In this book, not only will I share my personal story of my son's death, I will share with you my journey to acceptance, healing, forgiveness, peace, and living again. It is my hope that, if you are, or have been, in my shoes, that the words you read here will serve as a healing balm to your hurt, a guide through your pain, and an inspiration to the continuation of your life.

My family and I found a way to preserve the essence of my son's life. I offer the same hope to you.

Read on to discover how the beat goes on...

CHAPTER 1

A MOTHER'S WORST NIGHTMARE

I will never forget that day. Not only was I celebrating the release of my new book and overcoming my battle with a chronic lung disease, but Trevin was coming home as well. I was excited and looking forward to finally seeing my son after two months.

Coming home from work and sitting at the computer and putting the final touches on my book release event when suddenly, I heard gun shots.

I felt such a sense of unease. I couldn't identify why, so I tried to distract myself with other activities.

After a brief pause, I went into my bedroom to ask my husband if he had heard the shots as well.

He replied that he heard them, telling me not to worry. Still feeling uneasy, I went back to the computer to try to resume my work.

I had just spoken to my Trevin about an hour prior to hearing that sound. He was recently arrested and called after his release. Of course, I demanded to see him right away and he assured me he was coming over. When he failed to come by all day, I called him on the phone and he assured me that he was going to stop by within an hour or two.

Sensing my uneasiness, my husband Leroy also tried to distract me from my concern by sharing with me a text message from his friend who had reviewed my book. Just as I allowed a smile to creep across my face, a man came yelling and panicked outside our bedroom window.

"Hey, come quickly! Trevin got shot!"

I couldn't believe that someone was telling me that my son had been shot. They had to be mistaken.

We were given no details, just that Trevin was being rushed to the hospital and that we had to hurry because the situation was not good. I have seen the movies where upon hearing about a tragedy with their child, the parent experiences flashbacks of their time pregnant and in labor, scenes of the child's first steps and early words, or other joyful moments. I don't know if this happens with others, but for me, there were no slow motion scenes or background music. Let me tell you, my entire being just went into shock.

My body went limp and the room seemed to be spinning. I saw the little specs of light in my vision and almost immediately, I could not process my thoughts. I felt like I could not breathe. I did not know what to do, so I looked to Leroy to guide the way.

The night seemed a bit darker. It was like the dark of midnight, but without street lights. I felt weak, yet I knew I had to get to my baby. After getting in the car, in my mind we had already reached the hospital, but in reality we were on our way. It was if those moments had taken over me and I had lost all control. I could not control my crying, my silence, or my nervousness. It was so overwhelming that even as I recognized it taking over, I am still, to this day, only realizing the extent of the shock I endured.

The combination of this tragic emergency, the harried pace of the moment, and my own shock all conspired to create total chaos. I was simultaneously ordering my husband to go without me to be with Trevin, on the phone shouting instructions to my sister, demanding she come quickly, and yelling at my husband for trying to leave without me. I mean, it was mass confusion going on in my head and I felt as if I was having an out of body experience.

While the shock and chaos made it seem as if Leroy was taking forever to get us out of the house, the reality is that it must have only been a few minutes from the time we heard until the time we were in the driveway ready to move. As we ran out of the house, the man who brought us the news was telling us where to go, and my sister, who only lives a few blocks over from me, pulled up.

Trevin was taken to North Shore, a hospital

only two miles away. While under different circumstances, two miles is the distance of a morning jog or the short ride to the mall, during times like this, he might as well have been taken to the moon. I was frantic and nervous, my niece was in the back seat crying and even though we were five minutes away, it felt like an hour.

As we arrived at North Shore Medical Center, I remember seeing lots of people, a jumble of activity and a roped off vehicle. While I knew they were there regarding my son, they, frankly, were not my concern at the moment. I ran into the emergency room entrance and frantically asked for my son. The person behind the desk acknowledged Trevin was there, but claimed there was no other information. During calmer times, I understand that information is not instantly available across the hospital and a desk worker should not be responsible for giving out medical information, which may later turn out to be inaccurate, but at the time, the lack of information was incredibly frustrating.

Finally, in what I am sure seemed like a longer

time than it actually was, a nurse ran out and yelled to us that our son was being rushed to Jackson Memorial Trauma Center. So after the rushing and the waiting and the frustration, in some ways I felt back to square one as we were forced to take the long drive to yet another hospital, this one seven miles away from our present location.

As we rushed back to the car, I felt as if my world had shattered. My emotions began to take on a life of their own - one second I was crying, the next I was stomping my feet, and the next I was extremely quiet. My niece was in the back seat crying uncontrollably. My husband, Leroy, is a pillar, not only in the community, but in our family as well. Known for his works and deeds as the executive director of an organization and providing support to countless small businesses and individuals, he did what he did best, and seemingly held it all together. However, underneath his strength, I could see the look of fear and pain on his face and sensed his own shock, even though he expressed it differently than I did mine.

Due to the gravity of the situation, we were allowed to directly follow the ambulance which was transporting our son from one hospital to the next. Traffic moved out of our way, and we did not have to stop for red lights as we made our way to I-95 South and then off of 836.

To give you some sense of how shock works at times like this, I not only remember the ride as long and slow, but I do not remember the ambulance escort at all, even though we followed behind the red truck and flashing lights the entire time. I can only retell the story here, because my husband and family all insist it happened that way and that there was not a global conspiracy to block the roads and make it as difficult as possible for me to be with my son during his time of need.

My sisters and brother were calling loved ones the entire time, so as we arrived at Jackson Memorial Trauma Center, family and friends who heard the news were already there waiting, while some were arriving along with us and others were on their way. Rather than force me to go to the parking lot, Leroy dropped me off right next to the emergency room as he scrambled to find a long term parking space.

I rushed to the information station where the staff was expecting me, because family who had arrived earlier was inquiring on our behalf, and they explained that someone would come down to see us "momentarily." As you can imagine, I had no patience for that, I just needed to see my son, but every time I wanted to go up to where he was, I was not allowed. I was frantic, numb and void of understanding. My thoughts and my heart were racing and my mind was unable to either comprehend or accept my new reality - my son was lying upstairs with a bullet in his head, and I could not help him.

The doctors were unavailable to answer our questions, because they were in there trying to save Trevin's life. The only thing I could do at that time was to walk around in circles and watch family and friends watch me.

I'm walking, pacing, crying, and aching to know

what happened, wondering who did this and why they did it. None of this made sense to me, because I had just spoken with my son about an hour prior to the shooting. He seemed perfectly fine, and even as I played our recent conversations over in my mind, there was nothing to indicate that anything was wrong, much less any suggestion that this sort of tragedy was about to fall on him.

As we paced outside, inside and back outside again, I saw a few of Trevin's friends. After greeting each other, Leroy and I tried to squeeze some information out of them, but either they knew little more than we did or they were not talking because they were giving us limited information.

After what seemed like hours of this madness, a nurse finally emerged and called us into a small room where Leroy, my sister, and I were asked to take a seat. There were three others in the room: the nurse, a doctor and a man in a shirt and tie with a metal badge hanging from a chain around his neck. The badge read, "HOMICIDE."

The doctor shared with us that our son was in

extreme critical condition and because of the nature of his wound, a bullet to the brain, there was a low rate of survival. But even as the doctor spoke, even as he was finally giving me the information I had been demanding all this time, my eyes and attention were drawn like a magnet to that word: Homicide.

Even though I knew the situation was serious, and was frantic as a result, that word- homicide – which I heard countless times on the news, TV drama series, and the movies, jarred me to the core. Looking back, I can see that my response to the presence of that word is indicative of the extent to which I was in denial about what was going on, in spite of the wealth of evidence right in my face.

When the doctor finished speaking, I got up to walk out of the room. It sounds like a strange reaction, but the overall shock had me doing things that sound strange. I was emotionally exhausted, but I also think there was a part of my brain that was trying to protect my denial by not hearing the detective. Fortunately, my husband grabbed and sat me back down and the detective started asking his questions.

"When did you last speak with your son?"

"Did he have any known enemies?"

"Who was he with?"

I racked my brain trying to think of any and every piece of information I could give him, but I had some questions of my own. I needed to know who had done this to him and if the detective had any leads. Like many other crime victims, at that moment, I wanted whoever was responsible for this pain to pay with their life.

But my feelings were not just one dimensional. First of all, my religious convictions teach me of God's grace for sinners and the importance of our own love and forgiveness, even – especially - against those that trespass against you. In addition, more than a decade ago, my husband Leroy helped found *Brothers of the Same Mind,* an organization for ex-felons, and worked tirelessly fighting against police brutality, the criminalization of the black community and for job opportunities and other transition services for those ending incarceration and attempting to re-integrate back into society. I support that work and the underlying message: human beings do make mistakes, but deserve forgiveness and our support. And Leroy is a walking example of that message, as he evolved from a high school dropout and prison inmate, into a prominent figure in our community, a successful business person and the executive director of one of the most successful organizations in Miami-Dade County.

But this tragedy, which victimized my son, me and my entire family, was pushing me to the limits: the limits of my social views, the limits of my faith and, it seems, even the limits of my own grip on reality. This dilemma, when the realities of life crash up against the idealistic teachings of our parents, pastors and God, happens in every life, to one extent or another -- a stranger approaches and asks for help; someone walks past you and they fail to notice that money fell out of their pocket; someone transgresses you in ways big or small. Although we think it is, the dilemma itself is not unique or new, but how we respond to that dilemma speaks volumes about the

14

person and that person's faith.

After speaking with the detective, we turned to the doctor and asked to see Trevin. As we entered the triage area where he was located, I felt as if I had entered the gates of hell. There were all kinds of activities in the center of the room, from which Trevin was shielded by only a cloth curtain. There was so much noise from the machines and the teams of nurses and doctors rushing about and a smell that was faint, but left me feeling nauseated.

They pulled back the curtain and there was my baby, lying there unresponsive on a bed that was way too short for his 6'2" frame. His body, the same body I bathed and held in my arms when he was a child, was covered in goose bumps. He shook regularly from seizures and small amounts of foam escaped the sides of his mouth. As I touched his arm as only a mother can and assured him that everything would be alright, a single tear slid down his cheek. At that moment, I felt afraid and hopeless for my child. I felt like running as fast as I could, but I knew this was my reality and I had to face it. After a few minutes of staring at my son, I felt like I could not handle the scene any longer and couldn't bear to look at him. This could not possibly be my baby lying there unresponsive with a bullet lodged in his brain.

As stark and profound as this moment was, my mind was in such a state that I completely blocked out the memory. Believe it or not, more than a year after this scene transpired, I did not recall it and, instead, remained bitter at that poor doctor for *not* allowing me in to see my son. I remained convinced that the doctor refused to let me in to see Trevin and I still harbored resentment towards him for that refusal.

It was only as I began to research for this book that I revisited the chronology of events and talked with my loved ones about the details that they remembered about that horrible night. When I expressed my anger towards the doctor to Ramona, my oldest daughter, she thought I had lost my mind. "Don't you remember?" Mona implored me. "We both went up to see Trevin right after talking to the detective and spent an hour up there. You rubbed his arm and talked to him."

She was right and I began to recall the details of the visit. I don't know if it was part of the denial or just my brain's way of making sure I did not have a nervous breakdown by holding such a powerful thought in my mind, but that memory was completely suppressed until we talked about that day more than one year later. The shock distorted my sense of time, place and events.

I did remember walking out of the hospital that day, although my original memory was that I walked out right after meeting the detective and doctor, blocking out the hour I spent with Trevin in triage. I remember walking out to family and friends waiting for us, and how they gathered around me, and seeing the anxious look on their faces. As they began to question me, I could only form my mouth to say, "They shot my baby." My husband stepped in and gave the family an update on Trevin's condition.

My legs, my body, and my mind were tired from all the excitement. One minute I didn't want to move at all and the next minute I couldn't sit still. We were told to go home, that the doctors would continue working on Trevin throughout the night and we would be able to see him again the next morning. Realizing there was nothing more we could do, we left.

The ride home that night was torture. Leroy drove in silence as I stared out the window with tears rolling down my face. The trip was long and lonely, even though we were both there together.

Once home, we just tried to pull ourselves together and make some sense of this tragedy. While there was no way to make sense of it all, we knew that we had to be there for our son. But as I lied down to try and close my eyes, the noise in my head simply would not stop. My thoughts took a turn towards the vicious. The gunshots I heard the night before rang like bells in my ears as I tossed and turned in the bed. Confused and lost, I asked my husband what we were going to do. As he rocked me in his arms with the look of shock and pain in his eyes, Leroy simply told me, "Everything is going to be alright. Trevin is young and strong, so we will pray and trust God."

After a few hours of tossing and turning it was time for us to get up and head back out to the Trauma Center.

CHAPTER 2

BEFORE THE PAIN

Leroy and I first met when I was fifteen years old. He was my first love. We dated off and on over the next few years, but, as life would have it, we ended up taking separate paths. By the time Leroy and I reunited in 1996, I was raising my daughter and Trevin as a single parent. Ramona was twelve years of age and Trevin was four years of age. At the time, Leroy was raising his kids from previous relationships, which included Brion, his four year-old son. While two of his other kids went to live back with their mothers, Brion was locked to his dad's hips. When we decided to bridge our family together, we became a family of five, and I took on the full time responsibility of a mother to Brion. Boy was it rough in the beginning bridging our family! For

Leroy and I, it was great, but Ramona at twelve years of age didn't have much interest at that time to bond with her four year old brothers. As a matter of fact, the only thing she wanted at that time was to stay locked up in her room to be sneaky on the phone, or at least, she thought she was being sneaky. The only thing from that relationship she wanted was to get that bag of goodies from Leroy when he came home after closing his family store for the night. It wasn't until Ramona graduated from high school and started a family of her own before she took on the serious role of big a sister.

Trevin, as the baby was spoiled! With those big pretty eyes and chubby cheeks, no was a word he didn't hear often. Then Brion came along, who had the same issue as Trevin - spoiled! In order to keep their way, the kids would play Leroy and I against each other, which for a while, it worked. This went on for about a year until one day, I noticed a bond between the two boys. They had become inseparable. Yes, they fought from time to time and got on one another's bad side, but almost immediately, they would come back together. Trevin had become

Brion's protector.

Trevin was the popular one in the neighborhood, while Brion got tagged as the mischievous one. Whenever someone came knocking on the door, it was either for Trevin to come and hang out, or someone was coming to tell on Brion.

In this book you will not hear me say, that my son was an angel and that he did everything right. Who does? He was not by any means perfect, but he was a kind, caring, nurturing and loyal person. I knew right away when Trevin was born that he was special. The first thing I noticed was that his eyes were extremely big, he lacked pigmentation on his left side and it split right down the middle. From his waist down to right above his knee, front and back, it was a bit vanilla. I later learned that it was his birthmark. Up until he was twelve years old, whenever he had to see a different doctor, I had to explain to them that it was his birthmark and not the result of a burn. I remember he used to ask, "Ma, why is my skin like this?" I used to tell him that he was special. Eventually, as he got older, the color started to darken, but you were still able to see the difference.

It was such a joy to be his mother, watching him grow before my eyes. Time sure does fly. It was a couple of weeks left for school, and I was getting anxious. One day, Trevin got dressed to head out, but as always, hung around for a ride. While on our way, he asked if I was excited that he was getting ready to graduate. Of course I was, but I knew he still had an exam to take and pass, and since he had been so nonchalant about it, I told him to show me his graduation tickets, then I would jump for joy. So, before he got out of the car, he made me a promise that he would give me a call before twelve o'clock noon the day he got his tickets. He said, "Ma, when I get them, you will be the first person I call." As promised, he called to say he had his graduation tickets in hand, and they would be at the house when I got home from work. What I most remember about the day I received that call was that he sounded so proud to tell me he had those tickets. I must've called the whole family! On graduation day, he tried to act so unaffected but I knew he was excited, he hugged me and he asked me was I proud of him and he told me if it's the last thing he does he was going to make me the proudest mama in the world. And, as I think about it, he kept his word to me, I am still proud to be his mother.

Finally, his graduation was complete and it was time for him to head off to college. Trevin had enrolled in Miami Dade Community College. I was so proud. The time had come for him to report to college when I noticed that he did not head out that day to attend. I asked, "Why didn't you go to class?" He replied: "Ma, I'm going to take a quick break before I go. I'll register for the next semester." I was not a happy camper. A quick break! I reminded him that there are no quick breaks in life and that he needed to get up, get out, and make it happen.

About a month or so later, he came to me with four words and I knew it would forever change our lives. "Ma, I'm moving out." Again, I was confused! When had he been searching for an apartment? How would he pay his rent? But if I knew anything about my son it's that he was very responsible and he would never move out without a plan, good or bad.

With his newfound freedom came decisions that I was not always privy to, like his lifestyle, friends, etc. But he would always assure me that everything was alright. One day, while driving in the car with friends they were pulled over by the police, and from what I know in addition to a traffic violation, Trevin was also charged with possession of a gun which was found in the car. Trevin took responsibility for the gun and was arrested and taken to jail. My husband hired a lawyer for our son in this matter and after speaking with him, we felt like it was a case worth fighting. Trevin had been in jail for about two weeks before he had his first court appearance and I was sure that he would be coming home on that day. I could not go to court and see my son handcuffed and wearing "jail clothes", that's not how we raised him! So, I had to just wait for a phone call from my husband to give me the update. I was at work and pacing back and forth when I received a call from my husband. I could not believe what he had to say, "Trevin is going to serve two months in jail. He does not want to be on papers" meaning when he gets released, there will be no record and no probation. I didn't care about any of that, I just wanted my son home and I wanted to send him somewhere, anywhere where he could make a fresh start.

About two hours later, I received a call from Trevin. I remembered being so disappointed and trying to control my tears from fallen, but he had his ways of assuring me that everything was going to be alright. He explained as his father explained earlier that he wanted to come out of jail without a record and without probation. Yeah, that was Trevin, always accepted responsibility for his actions and he knew that he wanted to do something different with his life. Although he made some mistakes, I knew he was on a road to greatness just as I was after making my many mistakes. I just wish that he had more time.

There is a growing tendency in this society to turn people into the personification of one of their acts. For example, when someone commits a crime, in our collective minds, somehow they cease to be a father, a brother or a neighbor. They are converted, instead into a criminal. Not a father who committed a crime, but a criminal, a word used to encapsulate a person, not an act committed by that person. We must fight to remind ourselves that these are not criminals- they are our parents and siblings and children, who have lost their way. There is a term to describe complex human beings who have lost their way: children of God.

Like many others in the same position, Trevin did both good and bad deeds. For example, even as he was he could be surprisingly polite at home. Standing 6'2" tall, Trevin towered over Leroy, which makes for an unusual parent-child dynamic. Think quick: what do you imagine a "bad" child does when his parent chastises him?

Not only did Trevin not talk back to us, when being chastised by Leroy, Trevin would sit down so that he would not physically look down upon him. I am not saying Trevin ever did anything wrong or bad, but I am saying that he cannot be simply described as "bad." Trevin was a child of God. But this child of God was losing his way and having some problems.

As a result, Trevin was arrested several times for a range of infractions. Trevin was raised right and he never went without the important things in life. It is difficult for me to write and share this, but Trevin's temporary loss of direction was a major concern of mine at this time.

I want to make this clear: I did not love everything he did, but as my son, I expressed and maintained unconditional love for him. I did not have to choose between loving the respectful child or the one who got in trouble with the law, because they were both the same person and they were both my son.

CHAPTER 3

EMOTIONAL PURGATORY

The morning felt eerie and quiet and it was time for my husband and me to head back to the hospital. The doctor's had not given us an encouraging report the night before so I knew it was time to get a prayer chain going. Yes, our prayer mixed with faith alone is strong enough to reach the throne, but in times like these, I needed to mix my prayers with the prayers of others. So I called on my Pastor, my former Pastor, family, and friends to pray for Trevin's full recovery.

I knew it was going to be a challenging day, because there it was around 7 a.m. and I was already exhausted. My body was drained from crying all night, and my mind was exhausted from wishing I was dreaming. As we arrived at the Trauma Center, my husband dropped me off at the front entrance and he went to park the car across the street in the garage. When I approached the information desk, I was told he had been moved to the Critical Care Unit (CCU) on the third floor of the west wing building. Of course, that was the only information they were able to give and I thought to myself, this is good. I figured, if he was no longer in Trauma then he must have made a major progress throughout the night. Just as I was being directed where to go, my husband walked up and I shared what was told to me. As we went walking, I remembered asking him, "Why do you think they moved him?" He replied, "I don't know. Let's just get there to see what they have to say." From the Trauma Center to the CCU, I must have passed at least a hundred people and yet in my mind, I did not see any of them. My only thoughts were to get to my baby and get there quickly. Finally, after reaching the west wing building, we approached the elevator anxiously. I was nervously pacing the floor while waiting and angry because I was still waiting for the door to open. The door opened, we entered and, again, nothing but silence.

Not a word was spoken between my husband and me, but my thoughts were loud and were still flooded with questions. *Why did they move him? What did he look like? Was he in pain? What were the doctor's going to tell us?* As we reached the third floor, the elevator door opened and I thought I had walked into an operating room. Doctors and Nurses were everywhere. There were lots of patients and they all looked extremely critical. Some even looked as if they had already passed. This was not an encouraging sight for me. The nurse asked us who we were there to see, and when we gave our son's name, she called for the doctor to come in to speak with us. I was in no mood to talk! I just wanted to see my son! As the doctor approached, he asked, "Are you his parents?" We told him yes, and he began to reveal our reality in greater in detail. Trevin had taken a bullet to the head from an AK47, and because his brain went without oxygen for over five minutes, it was a high probability he would not be able to recover. I was shocked, scared and although I love God, I wondered, how could he allow this to happen to my child.

As the doctor's mouth moved, it reminded me of

an episode of Charlie Brown Television Show. When his teacher would talk, the only thing you would hear was *wah, wah, wah.* I could not make sense of any of it. In fact, the only thing that would have made sense to me at that time would have been to see my child alive and well. By this time, family and friends started arriving. As we went into the room, there he was yet again, just lying there. Cords and machines were everywhere on his body. At the touch, I remembered him being so cold, and shaking from those vicious seizures. I had had enough of looking at him lying there unresponsive. I was exhausted and I wanted so badly to rest, but all eyes were on me. They insisted for me to sit down, but before I could get comfortable, the doctors had a report. They explained, the human brain can only go up to four minutes without oxygen before the brain becomes severely damaged. By the time he had been transported to the first emergency room, his brain had already gone about twelve minutes without oxygen, which had put him in a brain dead state. In that time, there was too much swelling on the brain and it would have made no difference had they operated because once the brain cells die, you cannot get them back. As a mother, I wanted them to try it anyway, but we were told even if they would have been able to operate, things would not be good.

There it was a bullet to the brain and it would add more risk of life to remove it. I was told they were going to move him yet again, but this time to the Intensive Critical Care Unit (ICCU) and there he would have a chance to allow his body to fight. So there we were, getting ready to move to another floor and we were on a wait and see challenge.

In the meantime, a homicide detective came out and asked if he could speak with the parents. He told us that they had a few leads, but there was nothing concrete, and if there was any information we could provide would have been extremely helpful in putting pieces of the puzzle together. Of course, whatever bit of information we were able to gather we shared with him, but it didn't appear that we shared something he didn't already know. He assured us that he was working hard on the leads and he would keep us abreast. He expressed that it would be a good idea to do a press conference to see what leads we could get from it and I knew that probably would have been the best thing to do, but something in me panicked. I thought, *oh God the ones responsible for this will see us and gloat in what they had done.* I did not want them knowing any details of his condition. So my reaction demonstrated to my husband and the detective that I wasn't going to be able to do it.

As they were moving him to another floor, we were told that it would be a while before we would be able to see him because they had to set up his room.

It had already been a long day and we were just in the middle of it, so some of the family decided to go and get a bite to eat, but for the rest of us, we went to camp out in the waiting room. When we arrived, I thought to myself, *why is the waiting room so small?* I felt as if the walls were closing in on me. I needed space to move around and pace the floor. There were other families who had been there for a while, so a lot of the space had already been taken. We were able to grab a couple of seats, so we sat and the waiting was on.

Other families that were also waiting on a hopeful report regarding their family members in the waiting room were seeing my tears fall and with sympathy they asked, "Who is in there?" My sister, self-proclaimed PR agent, replied, "Their son was shot in the head and they are working on him." Of course, that opened the door for others to start sharing their stories. One mother shared about her son being in a motorcycle accident and his prognosis seemed as bad as my son's. Because of his injuries, they had declared him brain dead. Another family spoke about their son being shot in the Virgin Island and had to be air-lifted to have a chance of survival.

I bonded with them all, but not as much as with the elderly Hispanic couple whose son was a seemingly healthy young man, but suddenly suffered a brain aneurism. We were the first families to arrive at the waiting room every morning. For two weeks, we would gather and give each other updates on our sons' conditions. We were even able to get a few laughs in here and there as we swapped stories and engaged in conversation. Even after their son recovered and was moved to a different floor, they continued to pay me a visit and check on my son. I'll never forget them.

After about an hour of sitting and waiting, the doctors came in to escort us to where Trevin was. The beeps from the machines were as loud as a bull dozer in my ears and the nurses' station were full of doctors and nurses, and all I could think to myself was, this is bad.

As we approached Trevin's room and as I saw him lying there, something in me immediately shut down. Strangely, the whole while I was waiting in the waiting room area the only thing I wanted was to be in his room to see him and I was thinking that no one was going to be able to pull me away from him, but when I saw him my only thought was to get the hell out of there. Now, you may wonder, how could she not want to be there during that critical time for her son? Well here it is - the pain was overwhelming and I could not handle it.

Anger swept over me and the questions were

pounding my mind. Who did this and why did someone do this? I had to get out of there and run back to the waiting room. Where did that pain come from within me? It seemed as I forgot everything. I wanted to talk with God, but I couldn't remember how. My faith had seemingly vanished and my entire being seemed empty. Here I was, the sister who has all the right things to say to others in their time of need, but could not find it for myself at such a crucial time. I could not find my God and in spite of all I was dealing with, I then had to deal with the feeling of abandonment from my God. Yes I said it, I felt like our Father of mercy and grace had turned His face to my pain and left me standing alone to deal with my tragedy. The only cry that I was able to let out during that time was, "God, why have you forsaken me?"

The next morning, it was time to get up and head back to face hell on earth!

CHAPTER 4

THE LAST BEAT

I had no idea of what a rollercoaster this journey would be.

Every day and all day for the next two weeks this had become our life. I've never felt so alone, sitting in that room with the bland beige walls, and the stark air that always seemed to be thirty degrees below zero. They had a mounted television in the room, but I wasn't in the mood to watch it. I questioned myself over and over in my head. How did we get here? How did this become my life? Everyday waking up, getting to the hospital by eight thirty because visiting hours started at nine, stopped for coffee, got to the waiting room to put my belongings down and then straight to Trevin's room. I had become a robot and all I wanted was for someone to wake me up out of that nightmare.

There it was the day of Halloween and we were headed back to the hospital. Everything about that day seemed so strange. The elevators had broken down. The families I had come to know were arriving later than usual. The air conditioner appeared to be broken. But, in spite of it all, I was amazed at the vigor and energy my husband possessed. His faith was unshakable and he had made it clear that no one was to show any signs of tears or defeat while in the room with Trevin. In the meantime, I sat in the waiting room listening to my family tell me that this would be the day that things would change for the better. We were going about our normal routing when about midday the doctors informed my husband and me that they were going to do a final test to see if there were any signs of blood flow to our son's brain. The night before, we left a small radio playing next to Trevin's bed so that he could listen to music throughout the night. After speaking with the doctor, strangely enough, my husband, who for the entire two weeks we could not get to leave the floor, stepped out to make a phone call. It seemed as if they were gone for hours to have

Trevin tested, but in reality it was no more than fifteen minutes. I got up to take a peek to see if I saw them returning him to his room, and when I saw them returning him, I sent my daughter to go and make sure that his radio was still in the room. Minutes later, my daughter came back in the room with her hands over her mouth and she seemed really nervous. Well, I knew something was wrong and I yelled at her to tell me what was wrong. She yelled out, "They have a code blue in Trevin's room." Before I knew it, I dashed towards his room and my sister and the nurses were all holding me back and trying to control me. My husband, at this time, had no idea of what was happening, because he was still downstairs. My sister was holding on to me and yelling for the others to go and get my husband. While my daughter ran downstairs to locate my husband, my sister and the nurses calmed me down and advised me that they had brought Trevin back. My husband had finally made it back to the waiting area when a few minutes later, the doctor came out to inform us that once again Trevin was gone and that he was declaring him brain dead and he was going to get a second doctor to confirm. It's important to note, once brain death has been determined, it must be confirmed by a second physician. My husband, with tears rolling down his face asked if there was anything else that could be done. In the meantime, my daughter was told that Trevin was gone. She passed out on the floor, and there was total chaos. Because we had formed a bond with the other families, they shared in our pain and were hoping for a miracle. Minutes had passed before the second doctor confirmed him brain dead, and just like that, it was all over.

CHAPTER 5

CHOOSING LIFE IN DEATH

Only moments following my son's death, my husband and I were called to Trevin's room to speak with a representative about donating Trevin's organs. While sitting and watching our son, again the question was asked, "Is there anything you can do to give him back to us?" After receiving a shattering no and just me wanting her to be gone, we thought for a quick moment what Trevin would have wanted us to do.

Trevin was a dear child. He was shy, sweet and yet one of the most generous people you could have met. He did whatever he could to help those in need and therefore, we knew he would not have hesitated to say yes.

The representative was extremely compassionate, empathetic and respectful. There was no pressure nor did she make us feel uncomfortable. She explained the process and left the decision totally up to us. Trevin was young and took good care of himself and we knew that donating his organs would give someone else another chance at life.

My husband and I made a decision to donate our son's organs. Although that was never a discussion with us prior to that happening, we knew our son would have been honored to help save the lives of others. You may ask, was this an easy decision at such an emotional time, absolutely not! However, the thought of him being an organ donor and giving others another chance at life out-weighs the painful thought of losing him as a result of a drive-by shooting. Afterwards, I stayed a couple of more hours with our son's remains as family and friends said their goodbyes. I headed off to prepare for his services while my husband stayed behind to be with him until his organs were ready to be donated.

Our son passed on that Monday, October 31 and we laid him to rest, Saturday, November 5, 2011. Ironically, November 5, 2011, was the scheduled dated of my book release party. That day went by in a blur, and although I don't remember much of it – it was the second worst day of my life.

After arriving home, the feelings of anger and revenge started to once again, suffocate my thoughts. I believe it was at that point when my focus shifted from the pain of what happened to finding out who was responsible for this great pain. I can tell you this, the love of God did not shed abroad in my heart during this time. All I knew was that someone had taken a precious gift from me and my family and if I couldn't have my child back then I wanted the ones responsible for doing it. My ears and attention went to the streets and I was not leaving until I got answers. I went against everything of which I am not and tolerated people around who I felt could provide me with leads in my son's case. I trusted no one outside of my family and friends during this time. I began to sink deeper into my pain.

CHAPTER 6

THE BEAT GOES ON

I thought to myself, if Trevin were here and saw me in the state I was in - sad, depressed and crying all day, what would have been his reaction. Did I mention, Trevin was a "Mama's boy?" Well he was and there is no way he would have accepted his mama drifting away and living life as if there was no hope. So it was time for me to give myself a reality check. After attending a few of Life Alliance Organ Recovery Agency's events, I was asked to share my story about the loss of my son and saying yes to organ donation. The more I shared my story the more I started to accept what was real – my son was dead. It was at that point, I began my healing process.

Not long after the death of my son, I received a letter in the mail. When I first saw the letter, I was afraid to open it, but I knew that it held important information about my son. As I began reading the letter, my sadness was overwhelmed with gratefulness. The letter had confirmed what I already knew, Trevin had given the gift of life.

"...Your willingness to donate will be a lasting tribute to Trevin and an honor to his memory. We were able to recover four organs for transplant. This act of kindness has saved the lives of four people who were selected from the national patient waiting list for organ transplant according to U.S. organ allocation policies. These fortunate transplant recipients now have the opportunity to lead normal and productive lives. Furthermore, other organs were used for biomedical research which will assist in the development of new treatments and promote medical advancement. These efforts can lead to improving the quality of life for people as well as saving many others..."

Little did I know at the time, my pain was for a purpose! After receiving the letter my initial thought was to the "killer of my son", you all thought you won by taking his life, but his death was not in vain. But, after reading the letter, I felt a sense of pride and it gave me great joy that I made the decision to donate his organs. Most importantly, I knew Trevin was smiling down on me.

Whenever someone would ask if I wanted to meet the recipients, I would reply with hesitation. Honestly, it didn't matter to me one way or the other. You see, it's what you would call, "bitter-sweet." On one hand, it's a reminder of my reality and on the other hand, my son saved lives.

A few months after my son's death, I was sitting home feeling kind of down and thinking about him. When I received a letter in the mail from the donation agency, I thought the letter was in response to a correspondence that I'd recently had with them. When I opened the letter I was surprised to find a letter from one of the recipients of his organ. At first I wasn't sure if I should read it, but I owed it to myself to help deal with my reality. As I starred at the letter, my heart started racing, my hands were shaking, and my mind went back to the reason behind this letter. Here is a portion of the letter I received:

"...For years I waited for a liver transplant and every year that passed I thought it was impossible. However, thanks to the Lord and generous people like you made the impossible possible. As the result I received the transplant and my life has changed for better..."

Almost one year to the date of my son's death, I was once again, going through the depressed stages of my healing process when my husband walked in the door with the mail in his hand. He was hoping that my spirits were happier than when he left, but my tears told him a different story. Not sure if the letter would cheer me up or make my emotions worst, he reluctantly gave me an envelope that was sent by Life Alliance Organ Recovery Agency.

Once again, I was just as reluctant to open the envelope. I did not need another reality check, at least not at that time. But, something deep down inside was pushing me to open the envelope. They got right to the point, "The enclosed letter/card is from a grateful heart recipient, his family and friends." I felt nervous, anxious, and afraid all at the same time, but I knew I had to pull it together. I looked at my husband and told him what was enclosed in the envelope and asked if he wanted to see it, but his blurry eyes told me that he did not want to read them at that time. So, I sat up and began to read. Half way through the first letter my emotions took over. The tears started again, my body felt weak, and I knew that I would not be able to get through reading them all. So, I tucked them away for the next day.

I got up around 6AM the following morning with the letters on my mind. I brewed a fresh pot of coffee and pulled out the letters. I prayed "Lord give me the strength to be able to read them all." As I sipped on my cup of coffee, I began to start reading the first letter again at the beginning.

Here are excerpts from some of them:

49

"First and foremost, thank you is such a small word for the gift of life you so unselfishly gave us when we had no hope for the future..."

"As we start this letter, we know how deeply hard it must have been to make the decision that you made in giving the gift of life... Because of you, this man our children call Papa Don has been able to watch our middle daughter graduate from high school..."

"...After being on the heart transplant waiting list for over four months, my grandfather received the gift of new life..."

"...If I may be honest, when I was told to write this letter, my heart started racing and my mind went blank. I will never be able to say "Thank You" enough times to your family..."

"...For many years, we watched our brother's health decline. We saw the battle etched on his face as he coped with the pain and fear only a gradual loss in health can bring. When word came that he had a massive heart attack and his wonderful, yet broken

heart was no longer able to do its job, we prepared for the worst. When we received the phone call that our brother was to receive a heart, our emotions and feelings are difficult to put into words. It was such an up and down roller coaster. We were so excited, happy, worried, and hopeful for our brother, yet so sad for the passing of another and the family making that decision. We prayed, and continue to do so, for all involved..."

Some of the letters made me laugh. Some made me cry and some even gave me hope that I would be able to get through this pain.

Organ donation has been my light at the end of the tunnel. I have met some of the most amazing people – some are organ recipients as well as donor families. Donor families are others walking the same path as me. They have experienced the loss of a loved one and made the decision to donate their organ. Amazingly enough, some are living donors - those who have given up a part of them in order to give others a chance at life.

When I remember my son, this is the impact of his life that I choose to remember. Because of the events leading up to his death and the judgement that others placed on him while he was living, this is the way I choose to remember him: giving, loving, caring, gently, and kind.

Organ donation is an amazing way to preserve the life of your loved ones, or even yourself. The staff at University of Miami Life Alliance Organ Recovery Agency broke down the myths of the process and gave us comforting knowledge about how a decision to donate Trevin's organs would preserve our son's legacy and give hope to other families who would find themselves in our shoes – praying and hoping for continued life for their loved one.

I'd like to share a few facts from their site here:

Facts & Myths about Donation

Myths about Donation:

If I am in an accident and the hospital staff knows I am a donor, the medical team will not try to save my life.

Fact: Organ, eye and tissue recovery takes place only after all efforts to save your life have been exhausted and death has been legally declared. The medical staff providing treatment at a hospital is completely separate from the donor program and transplant teams. This is both required by law and is part of ethical medical practice. The transplant team is not notified until the patient has died. In cases where the person is not a registered donor, the transplant team is only notified when his/her family has provided consent.

*Donation will increase the hospital charges billed to the donor's insurance and/or his/her family.

Fact: All costs associated with donation procedures are covered by the donor program. There is no cost to the donor's family or his/her insurance. The donor's family (or insurance) is responsible for the costs of all medical care not related to donation and for funeral expenses – as they would be in any case.

*Donation disfigures the body. It will not be possible to have an open casket funeral.

Fact: Donation does not disfigure the body. It is a surgical procedure performed in a sterile operating room. The person's body is treated with the same care, dignity and respect as any surgical patient. When bone is donated, synthetic prostheses are implanted to maintain skeletal structure. Skin donation may give the appearance of a light sunburn but in cases where there is going to be an open viewing, it is taken from the person's back and so it is not apparent. Donation does not interfere with funeral plans because there is no disfigurement and no obvious suturing.

*There are age limits on donation.

Fact: There is no age limit on who can donate. A person's physical condition and an assessment by the donor program staff at the time of death determine whether he/she can be an organ, eye and/or tissue donor. From newborns to senior citizens, people of all ages can help to save and improve lives through donation.

Quick Facts:

• The donation process may take 12 – 36 hours (sometimes more), due to the matching process and the delicate surgery involved.

• The selection of recipients is based on many factors. Working with the United Network for Organ Sharing, the organization that manages the national transplant waiting list, the procurement coordinator will contact the transplant center(s) of the recipient(s) who match the donated organs. There is no discrimination because of age, sex, race or financial status when determining who receives an organ.

• Donation will immediately change the life of each recipient and those who love them as organs are transplanted within 4 – 48 hours after they have been recovered.

• You will receive a letter four to six weeks after the donation with general information about the recipients.

• Donation will extend the value of your loved one's life. Studies have shown that one in three families who decline consent for donation regret their decision.

To learn more about organ donation and the impact it has, visit *http://surgery.med.miami.edu/laora*.

CHAPTER 7

THE EMOTIONAL ROLLERCOASTER

The Merriam-Webster dictionary describes anger as: "a strong feeling of being upset or annoyed because of something wrong or bad: the feeling that makes someone wants to hurt other people, to shout, etc.: the feeling of being angry."

To say I am angry would be down-playing my true feelings. The hopelessness and despair that comes with losing a child is suffocating.

In search of the truth, I lost myself. I allowed anger, bitterness, brokenness, depression and sadness to keep me away from my moving forward.

I had become emotional and wrapped up in my pain and I could not see my way out! I tried reminding myself that God is always good and He has the power to see me through, but the only thing I could focus on was the fact that my son was dead!

Whenever I found myself smiling or enjoying life, the feeling of guilt grabbed hold of me and punished me.

I can remember at my first book signing, just a few months after my son's death, I could not bring myself to enjoy the celebration of my book release. Yes, I smiled and was happy to see others come out to celebrate my accomplishment, but inwardly, I was hurting and feeling an emotion of guilt. My thoughts were, what right did I have to celebrate when my son was lying in his grave? I thought to myself, any caring parent shouldn't have the right to experience happiness after burying a child.

At that point, the battle was on for my sanity. In spite of me knowing if Trevin could have seen one tear fall from my eye, he would have done any and everything in his power to make me smile. I felt like myself nor did his killers have the right to enjoy life. If I wasn't dealing with guilt then it was depression.

I went through the day as if I were a zombie. When I went to work, I was tuned out to everything and everyone around me. Co-workers tried to comfort me and some even prayed for me, and as appreciative as I was, I was tune to everything they did or said. I would come home and rush to put dinner on, and afterwards, it was in the bed and under the covers I went. Going to church for me became less and less. I tried to convenience myself to realize that I had other children who needed me to continue on in life, but nothing I did penetrated enough to snap me out of my depression. Hatred was starting to take root in my heart and I started to take on thoughts of revenge, and not just any revenge, but the kind that says an eye for an eye. I became angry with God. I could not understand why He would allow me to experience a pain so great that it causing me to once again, contemplate suicide. My baby was gone and I felt as if I was hurting my other children and making them feel as if I was not grateful that they were still here with me. I just couldn't make sense of anything during that time.

While lying there in my despair and telling God how angry and hurt I was that He allowed that to happen, He whispered to me, "Forgive." I thought to myself, He could not be serious, right? After all, no one stepped on my toes or stole my cookies, someone had murdered my child. I needed answers from God and I needed Him to ease the pain within. I was trying to convince Him to let me wallow in my misery and asking Him to bring down His judgment in the worst way to those involved either directly or indirectly, I wanted them all to pay.

When I wrote my first book, I had a dream that inspired me to change the title from "Chasing Butterflies" to "Let Go and Let God." So, there I was asking God to deal with my offenders and wouldn't you know it, instead He started dealing with me. You see, in order for me to deal with the hurt and pain, I would have to release the hatred that I felt within my heart. I had to realize, my tragedy did not keep me from moving forward, instead, it was the way I had chosen to deal with my tragedy which kept me from moving forward. I realized I allowed bitterness to take root in my heart. Trust me, in order for God to lead and guide us to resolve our issues we must continually ask him to heal us. Otherwise, it will rob us of our peace of mind.

You may ask, even when we know it is right to forgive does forgiveness come easy. Absolutely not! Some offenses are considered more extreme than others, such as in this case, but I will tell you this, the outcome will be the same, without forgiveness in our hearts. It's important to know, we receive according to our faith. So, we have to pray and keep on praying until we get our break-through. You have nothing to prove to anyone other than yourself not even to God because He already knows you. If you are holding on to unforgiveness in any area in your life, keep asking our heavenly Father to heal, deliver and to create in you a clean heart and you keep praying until your faith lines up with what you are seeking. In my situation, I'm careful to continue to stay before God in this matter because if not, my emotions will easily stir itself right back up in the area of unforgiveness. I have to continue to fight the good fight of faith. I figure, why allow those who have already hurt me and have taking something so precious from me and my family, to continue to violate my life, strength, joy and peace. At the end of the day, no amount of hatred or bitterness in my heart will bring my son back.

Who has offended you? God has never failed me yet and if we serve the same God, I know He is good to you just as He is to me. If He will see me through the pain of losing my son, I know He will see you through, whatever offence you may be dealing with so release it because you are worth being free. Remember, it's about leaning on, trusting in and relying on our faith in God.

Some of us are walking around with bitterness in our hearts because someone has looked at us the wrong way. Or, they did not speak or cater to our needs. Do we really think walking around with that bitterness is going to make us better? No. God has too much in store for us and whether you agree or not, He is not going to release it until we line up and let go of the bitterness that we may be carrying. It's the small things we leave unchecked that hinder us, so let's be careful not to overlook the small offenses.

Letting go of bitterness can make way for God's love, gentleness and peace to rule in our hearts. When someone hurts you, you can hold on to bitterness and thoughts of revenge or embrace forgiveness and move forward. The choice is yours!

Losing a loved one is no doubt extremely tough to deal with, but I can tell you that losing a loved one to violence is even tougher. When death occurs as the result of violence – such as murder, suicide, accident, for instance – the unexpected happening adds more difficulties to the healing process.

Not only do you find yourself dealing with the devastating loss of a loved one, but also the torture that comes from knowing the cruelty of the circumstances.

Whenever we neglect the healing process, we limit ourselves from moving forward. I believe it's safe to say that everyone doesn't experience the same thing to the same degree, but we do have emotions that must be dealt with. Unless God performs a miracle, we will have to walk out the healing process step-by-step.

Normally, shock and denial are two of the first things a person may experience when tragedy occurs. Now that I look back, I believe those two emotions protected me from mental devastation......

Some people often feel guilt. They begin to think of things they wish they would or could have done differently. Sometimes in our lives when we say, "I wish I would've, could've, should've!" or "I wish I had done this or that," we must remember, things happen that are sometimes out of our control and we must not beat ourselves up about it. When a loved-one leaves and we fail to give them a hug or kiss, it's not because we don't love them, it's just that we don't expect it to be our last time seeing them, hugging or kissing them.

As the apostle Paul stated in Philippians 3:13, "...one thing I do [it is my one aspiration]: forgetting what lies behind and straining forward to what lies ahead. In spite of it all, we must press on! The enemy wants us frozen in time instead of pressing on to the place God will have us to be in our lives.

Perhaps you like me also experienced anger with your loved one. I was very angry with my son after he passed away. I found myself countless times screaming, crying, and yelling at him, "Why did you leave me!?" Yes, I know that wasn't his choice, but as I stated earlier, my emotions took on a life of their own. Wounded emotions have a voice and they react! I love watching the Animal Planet channel and I see quite often, stand clear of a wounded animal because they will react. My family and friends tried so hard to help me, but because I was so wounded and broken, at times, I became unpleasant to be around.

It's important to know about the grieving process and some of the things you may experience so that you won't be led by painful feelings. When a major loss occurs, this isn't the time for a you to make major decisions or to become involved with any issues that can affect your emotions.

Hold on tight, because this is a big one here! Being angry with God is quite common although we are afraid to admit it. I struggled with the fact of knowing that God is good, all-powerful, and full of love for us and yet, he allowed this to happen. Now, it's important to know, this is where Satan seeks to build a wall between God and you. He uses this opportunity to say, God isn't good all the time – but he is! That's the reason you're still here. Your life could have ended with grief, instead God is using your pain as a testimony to others.

James 1:12-13 says, Blessed (happy, to be envied) is the man who is patient under trial and stands up under temptation, for when he has stood the test and been approved, he will receive [the victor's] crown of life which God has promised to those who love Him. Let no one say when he is tempted, I am tempted from God; for God is incapable of being tempted by [what is] evil and He Himself tempts no one.

No matter what, God doesn't change! He is good all the time, and all the time he is good. There are some questions about why God allows what he does will never be answered. We just have to trust him in all situations, good and bad. I can tell you, being mad at God isn't going to help you. After all, He is the only one that can make you feel whole again.

People experiencing tragedy often go through stages of emotional expressions of sobbing and madness and sometimes when you least expect it. Even people who are normally quite unemotional may experience a great deal of emotion during times of loss. I encourage you to hold on and fear not because it will pass. No matter what, pray and rely on the Holy Spirit to guide you through, even if you just find yourself saying "Jesus!"

Depression, as well as physical symptoms caused by the emotional stress, can be a part of the process. But, you can't give up; you have to fight the good fight of faith and resist it! Do not allow anyone to condemn you in your grieving process. Because I had written a book titled "Let Go and Let God," people would try and tell me how I should and should not feel. Knowing what you know does not exempt you from feeling the effects of life! It takes more faith to go through something victoriously than to be delivered from it.

Do not give up! God has healing for your sorrow, healing for your pain, and healing for your spirit. If you are hurting right now due to a loss in your life, a new beginning awaits you. You may not understand it all, but trust God to work them out for your good. What Satan intends for your harm, God can turn around for your good!

If you find that your grief has become unbearable, don't be ashamed to seek a professional counselor, social worker, or pastor. God has equipped them to help you along the way.

CHAPTER 8

GONE, BUT NOT FORGOTTEN

Through this whole ordeal, my greatest inspiration has come from my daughter. While sitting and writing this book, she gave me some of the greatest tools to keep moving forward, and I am sharing them with you:

Do not be afraid of setbacks!

So many people define progress as finding it easier to smile or making it through the holidays. But then a bad day comes along and they feel as if the progress they made was in vain, not realizing that that bad day was a stepping-stone towards their healing.

One day while driving to work, my normal route had a detour. That detour led me right to the intercession where my son had been shot. I started shaking, the tears started flowing, and just that quickly, I was back in that dark place. Because of my emotions, I ended up going back home that day and never made it to work.

While lying in the bed, I remember praying really hard and asking God to give me the strength to be able to confront that intersection. About one week later, I made a decision to drive down that same street, and with much prayer, I did it without breaking down.

Take joy in the memories!

The look on his face was priceless. For about a year, my sons bugged me just about every day for a flip phone. They would always complain that I always bought them the old-fashioned phones. I would get the same speech whenever they would break or lose a phone, "Ma, you need to come up, nobody uses these phones anymore." They were referring to the *MetroPCS* phone when they first came out. Oh no, I did not bend not one bit. Besides, as I explained to them, I bought him and his brother phones for my peace of mind and not theirs. They had gotten to an age where I wanted to keep tabs on them at all times, and the rule to have the phone was, when my husband and I called, they had to answer or the phone was ours. By this time the flip phones were the new gadgets. I was able to look from our bedroom into the hallway to see the boys come in and out of their rooms. One Christmas, my husband gave the boys their gifts and when they opened them, Trevin dashed from his room going into his brother's room and he stood at the entrance of the door and can I tell you, Trevin had the biggest smile on his face! I mean, that face could have made a spot in the dictionary next to the word happy. To this day, remembering that look on his face that day is forever embedded in my mind.

Look for the Signs!

Just as I thought he was gone, there are his initials carved on the closet door. One day, my daughter and I were cleaning and moving things around in my home office, and as I looked up, there it was "Trev." I smiled and at the same time I said to my daughter, "when did this sucker write this on my door?" We laughed and started sharing stories amongst ourselves.

Perhaps for you it is a letter, a picture, or even a trinket, something that reminds you of your loved one. Whatever it is, allow it to remind you of the love and happiness during that time.

Our loved ones have passed on, but they will never be forgotten by those they left behind.

CHAPTER 9

LIFE DOES GO ON

One of the hardest things I had to learn after Trevin's death is this – just because my son's life ended, that didn't mean that mine had to end, and just because I move on and try to regain the normalcy of life, that didn't mean that I was reducing the pain of his loss or forgetting about him.

It would've been easy to have just wallowed in the depths of my pain and set up homestead in the basement of my depression, and as much as I certainly wanted to never have to face "normal" life without my son, I knew I eventually had to get back to life and those – my husband and children – who were still alive and loved me.

How could I go on without my baby? How could I ever be *normal* again, when what was normal to me had been completely rearranged? How could I laugh again without feeling as if my laughter replaced the pain of losing my child, making him an afterthought? How could it be possible for my life to go on?

Those were the thoughts that crippled me in my pain. I just couldn't fathom how I was supposed to go on with my life as if nothing had happened, as if my entire world hadn't been turned upside down *and* flipped a million times. Life had thrown me for far more than a loop, and gaining balance again seemed impossible.

But isn't that just life? Won't there always be situations that catch us off guard and knock us off our feet? It could be a splitting marriage, the loss of a job, or some unexpected tragedy, but each of us will always walk the road of emotional turmoil. There's just no way to escape. Even Jesus told us in John 16:33 that in this world, we will have troubles. It's inevitable.

So when trouble comes and shakes up our world, we have a choice to make. We can either stay stuck in the disaster, or face the pain, heal from it, and then move on. Moving on doesn't mean you forget, it simply means that you are strong enough, in spite of how much it hurt you, to still make the best of the life you have left.

None of us can control what will happen to us throughout our lifetime. What we can control, however, is what we do in the aftermath. Tough times, particularly the loss of a child or loved one, are not the end-all to the vitality of life, even though it certainly feels like death's companion. You may not understand why, and it may never make sense to you, but what it doesn't have to do is permanently stop you in the tracks of your life.

No words I write in this book will answer those questions of why your heart had to experience such ache, but what I can tell you is that life – your life – goes on. I know, because even after the tragic loss of my dear son, although it took me a while, I have found the strength to live my life as if Trevin was still right here with me. As he looks down on me from heaven, I imagine that he has to be smiling, because I didn't allow his death to be my death.

I am enjoying life with my husband, my children, my grandchildren, my ministry, my friends, and allowing God's plan for me to continue to unfold.

The beat of Trevin's heart goes on through the lives of those who received his organs, and my heart goes on, knowing that families have been spared the pain I had to feel in losing a loved one.

I say to you, from a heart of understanding and compassion, let your life go on. Let the memories you created, the laughter you shared, the plans you made together be the fuel that ignites your will to continue to live an abundant life.

God's plan and purpose for your life did not stop with the last beat of your loved one's heart.

In honor of the one(s) you lost, tap into the strength that's within you and make the beat go on.

A PRAYER FOR PEACE

Lord, help me to embrace your peace which surpasses all understanding. Give me the confidence in knowing you are always with me – even in my darkest times. Calm my anxieties; rock me in your loving arms; and assure me that all is well. I give you all that I am not and I receive all that you are – love, peace, joy, wisdom and so much more.

Renee E. Jones

You are strong, you are capable.
Pray, have faith and always
do your best.

ABOUT THE AUTHOR

Inspirational and strong-willed are words that impeccably describe Renee E. Jones.

At a disadvantaged upbringing, Jones became the target of bullies and developed low self-esteem. As a result, began to act out using drugs at the age of sixteen. It was not until her first real connection with God at the age of twenty-three during a suicide attempt that made her realize she needed to change.

Although there were times, when she encountered many obstacles and pit falls in her journey. Her faith and obedience never allowed her to stray too far away from Gods' calling. Little did she know, her journey had just begun.

Renee Jones is the founder of Women of Destiny Community Outreach, whose mission is to impact communities and inspire women worldwide. In 2011, one day after the release of her first novel "Let Go and Let God," her nineteen year old son was murdered in a drive-by shooting. After dealing with such tragedy, Jones has become a supporter and advocate of others who are forced to deal with the death of a child. In 2014, Jones created the Trevin D'Shawn Reddick Foundation. The Foundation assists young men and women on their journey to overcome peer-pressure and guide them towards a brighter future.

Jones is a, Certified Life Coach; Amazon Best Selling Author; Board Member of the University of Miami Life Alliance Organ Recovery Agency Medical Advisory Board on behalf of donor families; Co-founder of the RJT Foundation; serves as a Mentor with Big Brothers Big Sisters of Miami; and she also volunteers with the Miami Rescue Mission mentoring women to live their lives on purpose.

Jones is a proud wife, mother and nana.

And The Beat Goes On

Renee Jones would love to hear from you.
Please share how this book has helped you.

You may contact her at

P. O. Box 681734
Miami, FL 33168

If you would like to book Renee E. Jones
to speak with your group, please send your request
to: Ramona Jules

Connect on Social Media:

www.facebook.com/I Am Renee Jones
www.twitter.com/iamreneejones
www.instagram.com/iamreneejones
www.linkedin.com/Renee E. Jones

Additional copies of this book are available online.